I'LL HOLD YOUR HAND SO YOU WON'T FALL

A Child's Guide to Parkinson's Disease

By Rasheda Ali

ISBN: 1 873413 13 0

American address:

5840 Corporate Way · Suite 200 · West Palm Beach · FL 33407
Tel: (561) 697-1116 · Fax: (561) 477-4961 · Email: meritpi@aol.com

European address:

50 Highpoint, Heath Road · Weybridge · Surrey KT13 8TP, UK
Tel: (44) (0)1932 844526 · Fax: (44) (0)1932 820419 · Email: merituk@aol.com

www.meritpublishing.com

merit
PUBLISHING
INTERNATIONAL

I would like to dedicate this book to my boys, Biaggio and Nico, who inspired me to try to reach others with loved ones who suffer from Parkinson's disease.

I would also like to thank a number of people for their help and guidance, without whom this book would not have been possible.

God. For the hard work of Dr. Robert A. Hauser, my great friend and supporter;
Dr. Theresa A. Zesiewicz - what a brilliant title and helpful input,
Erica Mandelbaum - you're not alone, Lucie Ventura - for getting my creative juices flowing;
Deborah Seager - for your touching words;
Gene Evans, Marta Garrido and Sean King - thanks for believing in me;
Bob - my best friend and partner for life; Jamillah - my better half and biggest fan!
Thank you Lonnie for making this project happen.
Daddy, I love you dearly! Thanks for inspiring me to exceed and not give up!
Love you all, for this has become a dream come true.
Let's keep working to find a cure!

Design, Graphics, Cover illustration and Artwork by:
SMK Design

merit
PUBLISHING
INTERNATIONAL

Foreword by Muhammad Ali

For over twenty years now I have had Parkinson's disease (PD). Fortunately, my health has been reasonably good and I still do many of the things that I have always enjoyed. Even so, I am aware of how much this disease has diminished the quality of life I now enjoy.

This becomes especially evident when I notice how my grandchildren and even my adult children become perplexed as the "new" me evolves. For my children, the change has been gradual, but still the nuances of this disease are a challenge to us all. With my grandchildren, it's been more difficult. Even though I give them all the hugs and kisses they will allow, they find it difficult to communicate with me. They don't understand why my arms tremor or my walking is stiff and rigid or why I don't smile as easily as they do.

I know many grandparents and parents are frequently at a loss in trying to explain to children the effects Parkinson's disease has on a loved one. Hopefully, this book will serve as a guide to explain in simple terms a very complicated illness. In this book you will find scenarios that are common occurrences for those with Parkinson's disease. This disease is unique to every individual who has it. The illustrated symptoms discussed may or may not be present in your loved one, or may appear in varying degrees of severity.

Additional information on PD is available through local chapters of the various national PD organizations. Community based PD support groups can offer help as well. Most of these organizations have toll free numbers and web sites that are easily accessed.

Even though Parkinson's disease can be devastating for all involved, there is real hope for a cure, and the promise of better treatments and medicines are on the horizon. What is important is to never lose faith and to never stop living each day to the fullest extent possible. It really makes me proud to know that my daughter, Rasheda, has become an activist in this cause and has written this book. Through her good work, our family's search to find a cure for this disease continues and expands. Hopefully, her passion will cause others to join us in this fight. I wish all who find themselves part of this courageous battle, much luck and I send them my gratitude and love.

Muhammad Ali

A Message from the Heart

I am not an expert on Parkinson's disease but because of the importance of the relationship between my father and my children and how this condition has impacted our lives, I have studied as much as possible to learn about the condition.

Parkinson's disease not only affects the people afflicted with it; this progressive disease also involves family, partners, friends and others. The fight against PD is a group effort that can only be effective when everyone is working together. You can better understand what your loved one may be experiencing if you educate yourself and your family about the condition.

Children should especially be helped to understand why their loved one with Parkinson's is behaving in a certain way. Because most children are curious, you will want to reassure them that their loved one is the same person they have always known. There is nothing to be frightened of and although their loved one may display some unusual behavior, they are the same as they have ever been with a small difference – they have Parkinson's disease. This book will help to explain to children what that means. It is my hope, too, that adults reading along with them will also learn something from the information provided.

For many years, clinical research has attempted to answer the often asked question, "Why did I get Parkinson's disease?" Scientists continue to study the relationship between Parkinson's and heredity, aging and environmental factors. Only about 5% of individuals with PD know of an affected first-degree relative and there is interest in whether exposure to toxins might cause Parkinson's. However, Parkinson's disease is not contagious and with treatment, many of the symptoms can be controlled.

Sometimes, patients with PD may feel depressed. As time goes on, they will become familiar with the signs and symptoms of their illness and this is where you have a big role to play in their lives. You can help them to remain feeling good about themselves by maintaining communication and compassion. If speech is an obstacle, for example, there are body language techniques, such as facial expressions and hand movements that are useful to help you communicate and maintain strong contact.

Be sure to walk with them through their struggle. Try to understand their occasional frustration and entertain them with pictures, arts and crafts or other hobbies you can enjoy together. Laugh together, call them on the telephone and visit as often as possible. Try, also, to help the caregiver at home because this job can be very difficult and challenging at times.

As the disease progresses, it may be more difficult to take on the added responsibility for your loved one – don't give up. They need you. Take breaks for yourself to relax and if possible, get additional help to alleviate some of the strain. Don't try to be a hero and make yourself ill with stress because in your loved one's mind, you are already a hero.

Some day, I hope to read a headline in the newspapers that says: "A Cure For Parkinson's Disease Has Been Discovered!" Keep believing and don't lose faith.

Muhammad and Rasheda Ali. *Photo by Gene Kilroy.*

How to use this book:

1 Read the text and study the illustration with the child or children. Each illustration reflects the symptom listed at the top of each page and displays a typical scenario of family life with a Parkinson's disease patient.

2 Suggestions have been made under the heading, *Speaking With Your Child*, to encourage dialogue with the child/children about the symptoms they are seeing in their loved one.

3 Try to explain more about the disease by using the pictures and the *Facts* included at the bottom of each page.

Children want to understand why their loved ones behave a certain way. By encouraging communication between them and your loved one with Parkinson's disease, you are not only educating them, you are also bringing them closer together.

Contents

Tremors

Most of the time, my Dad's hands shake a lot. I love to play baseball with my Dad, and it seems like his hands don't shake as much when he plays baseball with me.

SPEAKING WITH YOUR CHILD:

Do you notice your Dad's hands shaking? Does he shake a little or a lot?
Do you know why?

FACTS:

*Tremors are the most common feature of Parkinson's disease. Tremors are usually present when the limb is at rest. They may be present in one or more limbs. They may go away or you may not notice them as much during exercise or activity and during sleep. Tremors are not to be confused with *dyskinesia, which could be a side-effect of certain medications.

GLOSSARY WORDS:

Tremors - When certain body parts, like the hands, shake back and forth or tremble without contro
Dyskinesia - Involuntary twisting and turning movements of the limbs, mouth, tongue or jaw.

Genetics

I wonder if I will get Parkinson's disease just like Grandma. My mom told me that Grandma's sickness hardly ever gets passed on in families so I probably won't get it, even though I'm her grandson.

FACTS:

For years, doctors have studied the relationship between people who have Parkinson's disease and family members. There is a family history of Parkinson's disease in 5-10% of patients.

GLOSSARY WORD:

Genetics - Inherited similarities among members of the same family. For example, passing on the same characteristics such as hair color or eye color, from one generation to the next.

Shuffle Walk - *(Bradykinesia)*

Sometimes Grandma holds Grandpa's arm as he takes small steps. She reminds him to pick his feet up off the ground. I told Grandpa 'Be careful, I'll hold your hand so you won't fall'.

SPEAKING WITH YOUR CHILD:

Do you know why Grandpa walks in tiny steps?

FACTS:

As the patient's disease gets worse, it may be more difficult for the muscles to work with one another. It is caused by delayed transmission signals from the brain to the muscles. It is important for the caregiver to ensure that balance is maintained to avoid falls.

GLOSSARY WORD:
Bradykinesia - Slowness in voluntar
movements such as walking, standing
up and sitting down.

Stooped Posture

Sometimes when my Grandma is standing, I think she is going to fall because she leans forward so much. So I tell her to sit down. Mom always reminds her to stand up straight.

Slurred Speech

I don't always understand Grandma when she calls to speak with us. Sometimes I hear her very clearly but other times, I don't understand what she is saying at all.

FACTS:

PD patients exhibit speech or voice abnormalities. These may include reduced volume, diminished *articulation, hoarseness and variations in tone. These may be caused by rigidity of facial muscles, loss of motor control and impaired breath control.

GLOSSARY WORD:
*Articulation - Ability to form words clearly.

Depression

My family and I wanted to go out for ice cream and I asked Grandad to come with us but he said that he was not in the mood to go with us. He looked sad and I wanted to stay home with him to cheer him up.

SPEAKING WITH YOUR CHILD:

Why do you think Grandad looks sad? What can you tell him or do with him to make him feel better?

FACTS:

*Depression is very common in patients with Parkinson's disease. It is estimated that as many as 40% to 50% of patients are affected by mood changes. Depression is caused by chemical changes in the brain. Medications are usually effective in treating the symptoms of depression. Depression can occur at any time during the disease.

GLOSSARY WORD:
*Depression - Mood changes causing sadness and gloominess.

Sleep Disorders

When I visit Grandpa over the weekend, sometimes he gets up in the middle of the night so I watch television with him or we'll just sit up and talk.

SPEAKING WITH YOUR CHILD:

Why do you think Grandpa gets up in the middle of the night? What kinds of cool activities do you think you could do with him when he cannot sleep? Do you feel bad for Grandpa because he cannot sleep?

FACTS:

Sleep disorders are common in PD patients both from the disease itself and from treatment. *Insomnia and sleepiness during the day are both common. Tremors, depression and leg cramps may cause the patient to wake up several times during the night interrupting sleep.

GLOSSARY WORD:
*Insomnia - Inability to fall asleep at night or stay asleep.

Masked Face - *(Akinesia)*

Why doesn't Grandma think my joke is funny?

Why does she just stare and not smile or talk a lot?

Is Grandma unhappy?

SPEAKING WITH YOUR CHILD:

When Grandma gives you a stare like this (show an expressionless face), what do you think she means to say to you? Does it bother you when Grandma stares into space? Remind the child that Grandma likes his joke but she cannot laugh like we do.

FACTS:

*Akinesia means lack of movement. A Parkinson's patient cannot always control facial movements or display expressions, this is known as "masked face". Patients still feel happiness, sadness or anger. There are medications that can help reduce the tight muscle movements in the face and relax facial expressions making it more animated.

GLOSSARY WORD:
*Masked Face - Akinesia
- Little or no facial expression.

Diet & Medicine

I love it when we have big family dinners. When Grandma comes over to see us, she always lets me count her medicine before she takes it and she tells me what she takes to help her feel better.

SPEAKING WITH YOUR CHILD:

When you get sick, Mommy gives you medicine so you can feel better, right? Grandma also has to take her medicine everyday so that she feels better. I give Grandma lots of fruits and vegetables because it helps her feel strong and well. What does the medicine do to make Grandma feel better? Can you count how many she takes everyday?

FACTS:

Treatment for PD is very individualized and depends on the person and stage of the disease. The goal of medication is to control the symptoms of PD. Eating a healthy *diet with increased fiber, fruits and vegetables is important to general wellbeing. It is possible that the patient may be prescribed a new medication if the old one does not work any more.

GLOSSARY WORD:
*Diet - Food that a person regularly eats.

My Mom always cooks lots of fruits and vegetables so everybody, especially Grandma, stays healthy.

Exercise

My Mom has always been a runner, even after she found out that she had Parkinson's disease. Her doctor told her that she should still find time to run, swim or jog to stay healthy and strong.

I like to run with her even though she can always beat me.

Balance - *(Postural Instability)*

I did well in school so my Dad took me to the amusement park and he held my balloons so I could go on a very high roller coaster. Dad isn't able to walk for a really long time so he brought his walker and we stayed there all day...

What does the walker do for Dad? Did you know that Dad has a hard time putting on his socks? Why do you think he has a difficult time getting up from the couch?

FACTS:

Poor balance is due to impairment or loss of the *reflexes that adjust posture in order to maintain balance. This occurs more often during the late stages of Parkinson's disease. Balance problems can be dangerous so walking aids are needed to prevent a serious fall.

GLOSSARY WORD:
***Reflexes** - Spontaneous reactions the body uses to protect itself.

...Sometimes it's hard for
Dad to move around easily at
home and hard to
get up off the couch.

Motor Block - *(Freezing)*

When I walk with my Grandpa, he sometimes stops outside of the door before he walks through it. My Mom tells me to whistle and then Grandpa can walk through the door. He calls me his big helper.

SPEAKING WITH YOUR CHILD:

Why do you think Grandpa stops or freezes before he walks through a door? Did you know that you can help him go through the door? What kinds of things do you think you can do to help Grandpa?

FACTS:

It is not unusual for PD patients to find it hard to walk through doorways. PD patients have difficulty initiating and executing movement such as walking over a threshold. Have Grandpa try marching rather than walking when he gets stuck to see if this helps. You might also try gently tapping on his foot or using a laser pen as a guide.

GLOSSARY WORD:
Motor Block - To freeze in place before making a movemen This will happen most often when walking through a doorwa changing directions or turning around.

Stopping in place

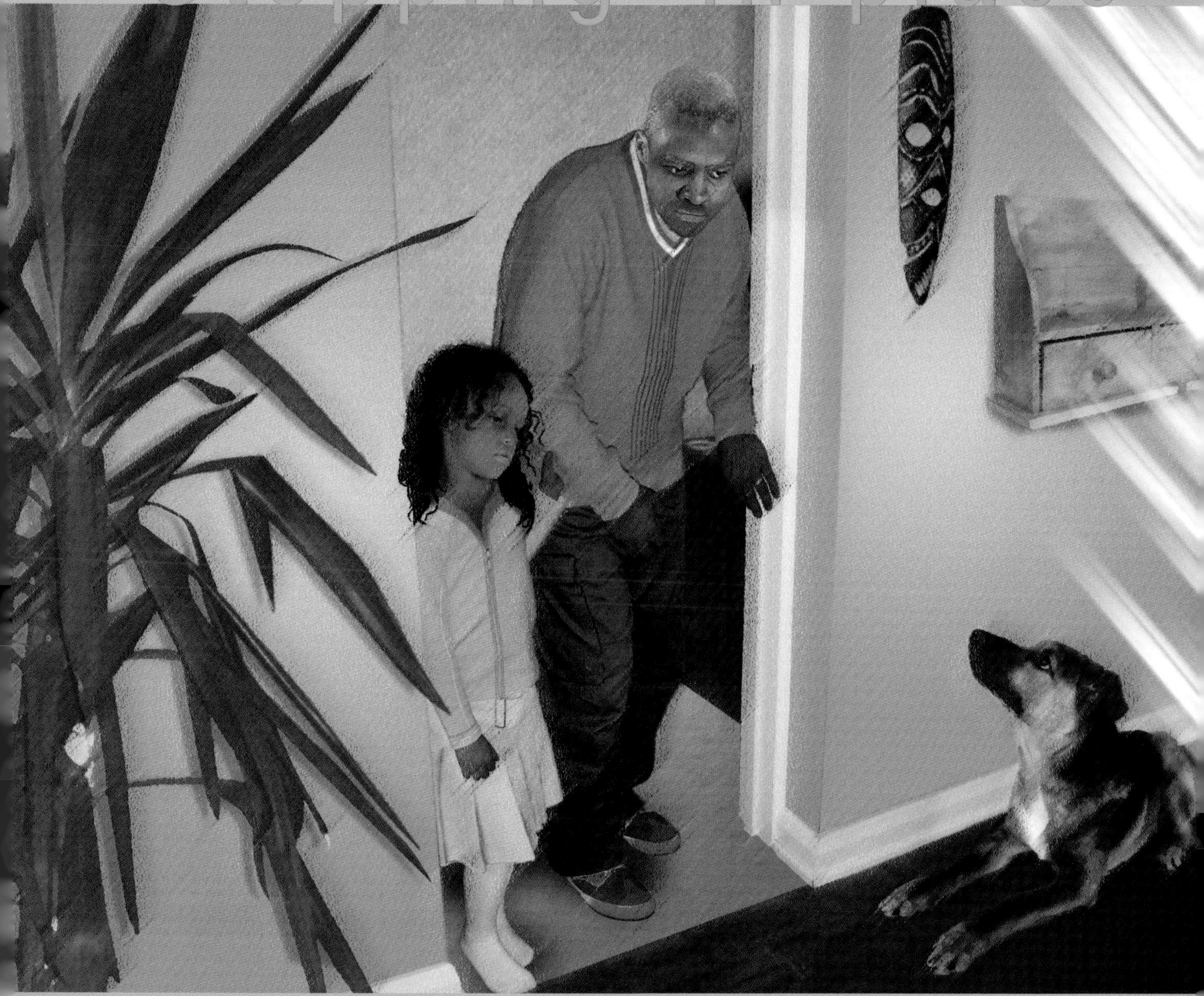

Early Stages of Parkinson's Disease

My Mom is a teacher and she teaches a lot of students at a really big school. She has Parkinson's disease but I don't notice it at all. She doesn't look like she has a disease.

SPEAKING WITH YOUR CHILD:

Do you think there is anything wrong with Mom? Did you know that Mom can teach for a long time even though she has *Parkinson's disease?

FACTS:

In the early stages of Parkinson's disease, the patient may not see any signs of the disease but symptoms will become more noticeable as the disease progresses. Sometimes, an early sign of PD may be a tremor of the hand where the person may feel the shaking inside without any outward sign. Many people with Parkinson's disease do very well for years before symptoms are troublesome. The signs of illness and how quickly they develop depend on the individual.

GLOSSARY WORD:

*Parkinson's disease - Disease of the nervous system that gets worse over time. The main symptoms are tremor, slowness and stiffness.

Hand Dexterity & Rigidity - *(Micrographia)*

We love to watch Grandpa draw pictures for us. Mom says that Grandpa cannot move his hands that easily but can draw pictures very well. We buy Grandpa lots of paper and markers so he can draw for us.

SPEAKING WITH YOUR CHILD:

The next time that we go to visit Grandma and Grandpa, we should bring Grandpa paper and markers. What kinds of pictures can you make for him? What kinds of pictures does he like to make for you? Why do you think that it is important for Grandpa to draw pictures?

FACTS:

Parkinson's disease patients can experience a change in handwriting, with the letters gradually becoming smaller and more condensed.

GLOSSARY WORDS:

Hand Dexterity - Ability to move your hand freely. **Rigidity** - When your body parts like your hands or legs, for example, cannot bend. They are stiff or hard and cannot move easily. **Micrographia** - Small handwriting.

Difficulty Swallowing - *(Dysphagia)*

My Grandpa has a hard time swallowing his pills so Grandma mixes them with ice cream. I told Grandpa that I love ice cream so Grandma gave me some too.

FACTS:

Difficulty in swallowing is common in Parkinson's disease patients. Patients describe a choking sensation along with difficulty swallowing foods. Parkinson's disease can cause a dysfunction in the *esophagus and abnormalities in swallowing. It may help to crush the medicine and mix with ice cream or other foods to make it easier to swallow the pills.

GLOSSARY WORD:
*Esophagus (gullet) - Connecting muscular tube from the throat to the stomach.

Brain Surgery - *(Deep Brain Stimulation)*

My Mom just had an operation on her brain and is now doing much better. Her hands don't shake as much as before, she is walking a lot better and I think she is a lot happier...

SPEAKING WITH YOUR CHILD:

Did you know that your brain tells all of your body parts what to do? When your Mom had surgery, the doctor put a small device in her brain to tell her hands to stop shaking. How do you think the doctor does that? Are you happy that your Mom's hands don't shake so much? What do you think she will be able to do with her hands now that she could not do before the surgery?

FACTS:

There are several types of surgery available for PD patients. One is *Deep Brain Stimulation in which a wire is placed in the target area of the brain and activated by an electrical current. This type of surgery can improve the symptoms of Parkinson's disease, such as tremors.

GLOSSARY WORD:

*Deep Brain Stimulation (DBS) - A type of brain surgery that uses a wire in the brain and electrical current to reduce the signs of tremor.

...I'm really glad I can see her laugh again.

How can you make a difference?

How can you be an excellent support for Grandpa or Grandma?

- Laugh a lot and keep a positive outlook on life
- Learn as much as you can about Parkinson's disease, so you know why Grandpa or Grandma do certain things
- Let Grandma or Grandpa show their independence as much as possible
- You can help exercise with Grandpa or Grandma - it's a fun activity that you can do together as a family.

What does Grandma or Grandpa have to do everyday?

- Exercise
- Eat nutritious foods - (Increase fiber, fruits, and vegetables included in all well-balanced meals)
- Rest and relaxation
- Take medicine on a regular schedule.

How can you make a difference as a caregiver in your loved one's life?

- Keep a positive mental outlook
- Find a qualified Parkinson's disease specialist with a lot of experience
- Support research
- Encourage physical and speech therapy
- Participate in an exercise program enjoyable to your loved one
- Ensure that there is enough rest and relaxation in their life
- Keep stress away as much as possible
- Explore new treatments and medications
- Join a Parkinson's disease support group
- Assist in medicine administration -
  (Make sure your loved one takes the correct number of medicines at the proper times).